Education Online

America's 100 Most Affordable Online
Undergraduate Degree Programs

Paul Casasus

ISBN: 1453822747
ISBN-13: 9781453822746

For Rosemarie and my Emma Rose

"It is never too late to be what you
might have been."

– George Eliot

Introduction

Not unlike many adults, my desire to earn a college degree would come later in life. Unfortunately, like so many of those adults, work and family were a priority that made that desire seem a bit out of reach. It wasn't until 1997 after speaking with a friend that I learned about online education. He told me that he was taking classes online at a local community college in an effort to earn his associate degree. I couldn't believe I'd never heard of this before. I was so excited about the possibility of earning my degree that I immediately began researching this particular program. I would begin attending classes online at this school the following semester.

Between work and my studies I began contemplating furthering my education beyond the associate level. However, my research only turned up a few schools that offered affordable online degrees, but in fields I was less than interested in. I began looking closer and soon I was looking at every school in the United States that had a website. Little by little I began finding schools that were both affordable and that offered programs I was interested in, but these schools were few and far between. I have yet to find a comprehensive list of affordable, online regionally accredited undergraduate degrees until I decided to write it myself. This book is a product of my frustration and desire to make the next student's research into online education that much easier.

Now, I have nothing against the traditional classroom, but as a working adult attending school in this manner was an improbable solution to a resolute desire to achieve an educational goal. Online education offered me flexibility and convenience that the traditional classroom could never afford. Today, nearly all public institutions in the U.S. offer some type of online coursework, either through fully online courses, independent study or the combination of the two, often referred to as hybrid courses. "According to the National Center for Education Statistics (NCES), the number of students enrolled in at least one distance education course increased significantly between 2002 and 2006, from 1.1 million to 12.2 million and the growth spurt doesn't seem to be slowing down" (http://www.braintrack.com/online-colleges/articles/online-education-continues-to-grow). Many believe that the number of students enrolled in online courses will move beyond the 20 million mark within the next five years.

Being able to attend school at any time, from whatever location you may be, is for many the difference between being able to earn a college degree or not. As a result, more students are taking advantage of online learning options, particularly at two year colleges and institutions offering associate degrees. However, growth is also steadily increasing in bachelor and graduate level programs. Studies on online education indicate that "instruction online improves student achievement, and that it is less expensive for students and educators alike" (http://www.citytowninfo.com/career-and-education-news/articles/growth-of-online-education-slows-but-its-future-remains-rosy-09100201). And in a recent U.S. Department of Education study, researchers found that students who took all or part of their class online performed better on average than those, taking the same course through traditional face-to-face instruction.

Although I have no doubt that you will find the information in this book accurate it should be utilized as a guide only. I wouldn't be surprised to find that many schools have either changed their tuition rates or made changes to their degree requirements by the time this book goes to print. So, please do your due diligence and research the school you hope to attend and its programs to gain a more accurate account. Although we posted only a minimal number of schools' military tuition rates, military service members should be relieved to know that several schools offer special tuition rates for those on active duty, so please be sure to inquire. We'll be sure to place more emphasis on those rates in our next edition.

The information regarding school programs and tuition rates were last confirmed during the month of August 2010. All schools listed in this book are regionally accredited by one of seven regional accrediting agencies recognized by the Council for Higher Education Accreditation (CHEA) http://www.chea. org/Directories/regional.asp. Regional accreditation is considered the premier standard of college accreditation. It is the most widely recognized type of accreditation and the most accepted in terms of transferring credits and degrees.

I am currently in the process of writing another book in similar fashion regarding affordable, online regionally accredited graduate degrees, which should be completed by the Spring of 2011. So, please keep an eye out for that. I hope this book proves beneficial and helps in whatever educational endeavors you may partake. Good luck to you all.

Acknowledgments

From North Carolina A&T State to Colorado State University the journey has been long but tremendously rewarding. I'm hopeful that the time and effort put forth on this project will culminate in the procurement of educational advancement for many students to come.

This book is dedicated to my life's partner, Rosemarie Gallegos and my daughter Emma Rose. You two are all the inspiration I need. Thank you for your unwavering support and for accepting the role, among others, of sounding board for my ideas.

I would love to hear from you. If you have any positive stories, anecdotes, suggestions, feel your alma mater should have made the list, or would like to point out any discrepancies, please contact me at chataboutbook@gmail.com. I look forward to your comments.

Contents

List of colleges and universities with distance education programs in ranked order as covered in the text.

North Carolina A&T State University   (1)

1601 E. Market Street
Greensboro, NC 27411
(336) 334-7946
Website – www.ncat.edu

Accreditation: Southern Association of Colleges and Schools.
www.sacs.org

Type of program offered online: Bachelor / Master /
Doctorate
Programs accessible to students: Worldwide

Undergraduate tuition per credit hour online:
In state – $80.00
Out of state – $399.00

Undergraduate programs offered online:
BS – Agricultural Education
BS – Business Education
BS – Electronics Technology
BS – Occupational Safety and Health
BS – Technology Education

Fayetteville State University

1200 Murchison Road
Fayetteville, NC 28301
(910) 672-1111
Website – www.uncfsu.edu

Accreditation: Southern Association of Colleges and Schools.
www.sacs.org

Type of program offered online: Bachelor / Master
Programs accessible to students: Worldwide

Undergraduate tuition per credit hour online:
In state – $82.50
Out of state – $435.50

Undergraduate programs offered online:
BS – Criminal Justice
BS – General Business Administration
RN to BSN – Nursing
BS – Psychology
BA – Sociology

University of North Carolina, Greensboro (3)

1400 Spring Garden Street
Greensboro, NC 27412
(336) 334-5000
Website – www.uncg.edu

Accreditation: Southern Association of Colleges and Schools.
www.sacs.org

Type of program offered online: Bachelor / Master
Programs accessible to students: Worldwide

Undergraduate tuition per credit hour online:
In state – $87.50
Out of state – $175.00

Undergraduate programs offered online:
BS – Business Administration
BS – Human Development and Family Studies
BS – Health Studies
BA – Liberal Studies

Western Carolina University (4)

138 Camp Building
Cullowhee, NC 28723
(800) 928-4968
Website – www.wcu.edu

Accreditation: Southern Association of Colleges and Schools.
www.sacs.org

Type of program offered online: Certificate / Bachelor / Master / Licensure
Programs accessible to students: Worldwide

Undergraduate tuition per credit hour online:
In state – $89.83
Out of state – $378.05

Undergraduate programs offered online:
BS – Birth-Kindergarten
BS – Criminal Justice
BS – Emergency Medical Care
BS – Emergency and Disaster Management
BS – Health Information Administration *
RN to BSN – Nursing
Certificate – Culturally Based Native Health
Certificate – Financial Planning and CFP Exam Prep
Licensure – AIG (Academically or Intellectually Gifted)

* Online degree program for Registered Health Information Technician's (RHITs).

North Carolina Central University   (5)

1801 Fayetteville St.
Durham, NC 27707
(919) 530-6100
Website – www.nccu.edu

Accreditation: Southern Association of Colleges and Schools.
www.sacs.org

Type of program offered online: Certificate / Bachelor / Master
Programs accessible to students: Worldwide

Undergraduate tuition per credit hour online:
In state – $95.46
Out of state – $452.66

Undergraduate programs offered online:
BS – Birth to Kindergarten Education *
BS – Hospitality and Tourism Administration
RN to BSN – Nursing
Certificate – English Language Development
Certificate – Recreational Management

*   Residency requirement.

East Carolina University (6)

East Fifth Street
Greenville, NC 27858-4353
(252) 328-6131
Website – www.ecu.edu

Accreditation: Southern Association of Colleges and Schools.
www.sacs.org

Type of program offered online: Certificate / Bachelor / Master / Licensure
Programs accessible to students: Worldwide

Undergraduate tuition per credit hour online:
In state – $100.00
Out of state – $466.00

Undergraduate programs offered online:
BSBA – Business Administration:
      Management
      Management Information Systems
      Marketing, Operations and Supply Chain Management
BSBE – Business Education:
      Information Technologies
BS – Communication
BS – Education:
    Birth-Kindergarten Education
    Business Education
BS – Health Information Management
BS – Health Services Management
BS – Hospitality Management
BS – Industrial Distribution and Logistics
BS – Industrial Technology:
    Bio-process Manufacturing
    Industrial Distribution and Logistics
    Industrial Supervision
    Information and Computer Technology

Manufacturing Systems
RN to BSN – Nursing

Wachovia Partnership East
BS – Elementary Education *
BS – Middle Grades Education *
BS – Special Education *

* Wachovia Partnership East programs utilize a part-time cohort model and is designed for students transferring from a North Carolina community college.

Winston Salem State University   (7)

601 S. Martin Luther King Jr. Drive
Winston-Salem, NC 27110
(336) 750-2000
Website – www.wssu.edu

Accreditation: Southern Association of Colleges and Schools.
www.sacs.org

Type of program offered online: Certificate / Bachelor / Master
Programs accessible to students: Worldwide

Undergraduate tuition per credit hour online:
In state – $114.78
Out of state – $418.36

Undergraduate programs offered online:
BS – Clinical Laboratory Science
BIS – Integrative Studies

Athens State University   (8)

300 North Beaty Street
Athens, AL 35611-1999
(256) 233-8100
(800) 522-0272
Website – www.athens.edu

Accreditation: Southern Association of Colleges and Schools.
www.sacs.org

Type of program offered online: Bachelor
Programs accessible to students: Worldwide

Undergraduate tuition per credit hour online:
In state – $128.00
Out of state – $255.00

Undergraduate programs offered online:
BS – Computer Science:
        Computer Information Systems
BA – Religious Studies

University of Wyoming (9)

1000 E. University Ave.
Laramie, WY 82071
(307) 766-1121
Website – www.uwyo.edu

Accreditation: North Central Association of Colleges and Schools. www.ncahlc.org

Type of program offered online: Certificate / Bachelor / Master
Programs accessible to students: Worldwide

Undergraduate tuition per credit hour online:
In state – $134.00
Out of state – $134.00

Undergraduate programs offered online:
BS – Business Administration
BS – Family and Consumer Sciences:
    Professional Child Development
RN to BSN – Nursing

Florida Atlantic University (10)

777 Glades Road
Boca Raton, FL 33431
(561) 297-3000
Website – www.fau.edu

Accreditation: Southern Association of Colleges and Schools.
www.sacs.org

Type of program offered online: Certificate / Bachelor / Master
Programs accessible to students: Worldwide

Undergraduate tuition per credit hour online:
In state – $139.55
Out of state – $584.14

Undergraduate programs offered online:
BBA – Business Administration:
>Accounting
>Management
>Marketing

Certificate – Gerontology

Weber State University (11)

3848 Harrison Blvd.
Ogden, UT 84408
(801) 626-6000
Website – www.weber.edu

Accreditation: Northwest Commission on Colleges and Universities. www.nwccu.org

Type of program offered online: Certificate / Associate / Bachelor
Programs accessible to students: Worldwide

Undergraduate tuition per credit hour online:
In state – $139.91
Out of state – $202.00

Undergraduate programs offered online:
AAS – Clinical Laboratory Technician
AS – General Studies
AAS – Health Information Technology
BS – Clinical Laboratory Science
BS – Health Information Management
BS – Health Services Administration
BIS – Integrated Studies:
    Child & Family Studies
    Computer Science
    Health Administrative Services
    Health Promotion
    Health Sciences
    History
    Information Systems & Technology (IS&T)
    Nutrition Education
    Production and Inventory Control
    Sales & Service Technology

Certificate – Health Care Coding & Classification

*   Some programs may not be offered fully online. Independent study courses may be part of some programs.

Florida International University (12)

11200 S.W. 8th Street
Modesto A. Maidique Campus
Ryder Business Building, RB Lobby
Miami, FL 33199
(305) 348-3630
(877)-3-ELEARN (335-3276)
Website – www.fiu.edu

Accreditation: Southern Association of Colleges and Schools.
www.sacs.org

Type of program offered online: Certificate / Bachelor / Master
Programs accessible to students: Worldwide

Undergraduate tuition per credit hour online:
In state – $142.04
Out of state – $555.34
Non-Florida Resident Program – $333.00 *

Undergraduate programs offered online:
BS – Criminal Justice
BBA – Finance
BBA – Human Resource Management
BBA – International Business
BBA – Management
RN to BSN – Nursing
BPA – Public Administration
Certificate – African and African Disapora Studies
Certificate – Paralegal
Certification – FIBA-FIU Certified Associate in AML (AML/CA)

Non-Florida Resident Program
BBA – Finance *
BBA – Human Resource Management *
BBA – International Business *
BBA – Management *

*   Non-Florida Resident Program. To be admitted to any of the Non-Florida Resident programs, students must reside outside of the state of Florida. Tuition for these programs is ($333.00 pch).

Eastern Oregon University (13)

One University Boulevard
La Grande, OR 97850-2899
(541) 962-3672
Website – www.eou.edu

Accreditation: Northwest Commission on Colleges and Universities. www.nwccu.org

Type of program offered online: Bachelor / Master
Programs accessible to students: Worldwide

Undergraduate tuition per credit hour online:
In state – $143.00 *
Out of state – $143.00 *

Undergraduate programs offered online:
BS – Business Administration
BS – Business / Economics
BA – English / Writing
BA/BS – Fire Services Administration
BA/BS – Liberal Studies:
      Business / Health Promotion
      Business & Psychology
      Early Childhood
      Environmental Studies
      Small City & Rural County Management
      Two Minors
BA/BS – Physical Activity & Health
BA/BS – Psychology

* Tuition is based on the quarter system, not the semester system. 1 quarter credit equals 1.5 semester credit hours.

North Carolina State University   (14)

P.O. Box 7103
Raleigh, NC 27695
(919) 515-2011
Website – www.ncsu.edu

Accreditation: Southern Association of Colleges and Schools.
www.sacs.org

Type of program offered online: Certificate / Bachelor / Master
Programs accessible to students: Worldwide

Undergraduate tuition per credit hour online:
In state – $147.00
Out of state – $281.00

Undergraduate programs offered online:
BS – Engineering in Mechatronics (Joint Program) *
BS – Engineering (2+2 Program) *
BA – Leadership in the Public Sector
Certificate – Agricultural Business Management
Certificate – Agronomic Crop Production
Certificate – Computer Programming
Certificate – Fabric Manufacturing
Certificate – Feed Milling
Certificate – Food Safety
Certificate – Plant, Pests, Pathogens and People
Certificate – Soil Science
Certificate – Textile Fundamentals

*   Residency requirement.

Western New Mexico University   (15)

1000 W. College St.
Silver City, NM 88062
(800) 872-9668
Website – www.wnmu.edu

Accreditation: North Central Association of Colleges and Schools. www.ncahlc.org

Type of program offered online: Bachelor / Master
Programs accessible to students: Worldwide

Undergraduate tuition per credit hour online:
In state – $149.66 *
Out of state – $149.66 *

Undergraduate programs offered online:
BAS – Career & Technical Teacher Education (2+2 Program) **
BAS – Criminal Justice
RN to BSN – Nursing
BA – Rehabilitation Services

*   Tuition per credit hour rate is an estimate based on a student participating in two courses or 6 credit hours. Please contact school for a more accurate account.
** 2+2 program is designed primarily for students who already hold an AAS, AS degree, or have 45 credit hours in an applied technology / technical area.

Adams State College   (16)

208 Edgemont Blvd.
Alamosa, CO 81102
(719) 587-7011
(800) 824-6494
Website – www.adams.edu

Accreditation: North Central Association of Colleges and Schools. www.ncahlc.org

Type of program offered online: Associate / Bachelor / Master / Licensure
Programs accessible to students: Worldwide

Undergraduate tuition per credit hour online:
In state – $150.00
Out of state – $150.00

Undergraduate programs offered online:
AA – Associate of Arts
AS – Associate of Science
BA – Business Administration
BS – Business Administration
BA – Interdisciplinary Studies
BS – Interdisciplinary Studies:
        History/Government
BA – Sociology
Licensure – Elementary Education

California State University, Bakersfield   (17)

9001 Stockdale Highway
Bakersfield, CA 93311-1022
(661) 654-2441
Website – www.csub.edu

Accreditation: Western Association of Schools and Colleges.
www.wascsenior.org

Type of program offered online: Bachelor / Master
Programs accessible to students: Worldwide

Undergraduate tuition per credit hour online:
In state – $150.00
Out of state – $150.00

Undergraduate programs offered online:
BS – Environmental Resource Management

University of Houston, Clear Lake   (18)

2700 Bay Area Blvd.
Houston, TX 77058
(281) 283-2500
Website – www.uhcl.edu

Accreditation: Southern Association of Colleges and Schools.
www.sacs.org

Type of program offered online: Certificate / Bachelor / Master
Programs accessible to students: Worldwide

Undergraduate tuition per credit hour online:
In state – $155.00
Out of state – $463.00

Undergraduate programs offered online:
BS – Psychology *
Certificate – Distance Educator Certificate
Certificate – Fitness and Human Performance
Certificate – Performance Technology
Certificate – 8-12 Technology Applications Certificate
Certificate – EC-12 Technology Applications Certificate

*   Program available Fall 2010.

Eastern New Mexico University (19)

1500 S. Ave K.
Portales, NM 88130
(575) 562-1011
(800)-FOR-ENMU (367-3668)
Website – www.enmu.edu

Accreditation: North Central Association of Colleges and Schools. www.ncahlc.org

Type of program offered online: Associate / Bachelor
Programs accessible to students: Worldwide

Undergraduate tuition per credit hour online:
In state – $162.50
Out of state – $162.50

Undergraduate programs offered online:
AA – General Studies
BAAS – Applied Arts and Science
BAAS – Aviation Science
BS – Aviation Science
BBA – Business Administration
BS – Nursing
BOE – Occupational Education / Professional Technical Education
BA/BS -- Religion
BUS – University Studies

University of Arkansas (20)

Administration Bldg 425
Fayetteville, AK 72701
(479) 575-2000
Website – www.uark.edu

Accreditation: North Central Association of Colleges and Schools. www.ncahlc.org

Type of program offered online: Certificate / Bachelor / Master / Licensure
Programs accessible to students: Worldwide

Undergraduate tuition per credit hour online:
In state – $167.00
Out of state – $462.91

Undergraduate programs offered online:
BS – Business administration *
BSE – Elementary Education
BSE – Human Resource Development **

*   Tuition for this program is (In state – $174.43 pch) (Out of state – $483.49 pch).
**   Tuition for this program is (In state / Out of state – $198.68 pch)

University of Arkansas, Little Rock   (21)

2801 S. University Avenue
Little Rock, AR 72204
(501) 569-3127
Website – www.ualr.edu

Accreditation: North Central Association of Colleges and Schools. www.ncahlc.org

Type of program offered online: Certificate / Bachelor / Master
Programs accessible to students: Worldwide

Undergraduate tuition per credit hour online:
In state – $167.75
Out of state – $450.00

Undergraduate programs offered online:
BA – Criminal Justice
BS – Health Education and Promotion
BA – Liberal Arts
BBA – Management:
    General Management
    Human Resource Management
BA – Mathematics
BS – Mathematics
BS – Nursing

Fort Hays State University (22)

600 Park Street
Hays, KS 67601-4099
(785) 628- FHSU (3478)
Website – www.fhsu.edu

Accreditation: North Central Association of Colleges and Schools. www.ncahlc.org

Type of program offered online: Certificate / Associate / Bachelor / Master / Specialist / Endorsement
Programs accessible to students: Worldwide

Undergraduate tuition per credit hour online:
In state – $168.00
Out of state – $168.00

Undergraduate programs offered online:
AA – General Studies
BBA – Business Communication
BS – Education:
    Early Childhood Unified
    TEAM Honors
BS – Elementary Education:
    TEAM K-6 with Special Education Minor
BGS – General Studies
BS – Information Networking & Telecommunications:
    Computer Networking and Telecommunications
    Web Development
BS – Justice Studies
BBA – Management:
    Human Resources
BBA – Management Information Systems
BBA – Marketing
BS – Medical Diagnostic Imaging
BS – Nursing
BS – Organizational Leadership

BA – Political Science
BA – Sociology
BS – Technology Leadership
BBA – Tourism and Hospitality Management
Certificate – Addictions Counseling
Certificate – Adult Care Home Administration
Certificate – Business Information Systems
Certificate – Cardiovascular Interventional Technology (CVIT)
Certificate – Cisco Online / Prep Program for Cisco Certified
Network Associate (CCNA)
Certificate – Community Development
Certificate – Community Health
Certificate – Community Health Promotion
Certificate – Computed Tomography (CT)
Certificate – Consumer Health
Certificate – Corrections
Certificate – Customer Service
Certificate – E-Commerce Web Development
Certificate – Emergency Services Leadership
Certificate – Geographic Information Systems (GIS) Use
Certificate – Globalization and Culture Change
Certificate – Grant Proposal Writing and Program Evaluation
Certificate – Healthy Aging
Certificate – Human Resources Management
Certificate – International Studies
Certificate – Internetworking
Certificate – Justice Networking
Certificate – Law and the Courts
Certificate – Law Enforcement
Certificate – Leadership
Certificate – Life Stages and Transitions
Certificate – Literacy Coach
Certificate – Magnetic Resonance Imaging (MRI)
Certificate – Management
Certificate – Marketing
Certificate – Operations Management
Certificate – Pre-Law

Certificate – Public Administration
Certificate – Reading Teacher
Certificate – Sociology of Medicine and Aging
Certificate – Tourism and Hospitality Leadership
Certificate – Tourism and Hospitality Management
Certificate – Tourism and Hospitality Marketing
Certificate – Victim Advocacy
Certificate – Web Development
Certificate – Women's and Gender Studies
Certificate – Women's Imaging *

*   Residency requirement.

Indiana University, Bloomington (23)

107 S. Indiana Ave.
Bloomington, IN 47405-7000
(812) 855-4848
Website – www.iub.edu

Accreditation: North Central Association of Colleges and Schools. www.ncahlc.org

Type of program offered online: Diploma / Associate / Bachelor
Programs accessible to students: Worldwide

Undergraduate tuition per credit hour online:
In state – $169.51
Out of state – $197.06

Undergraduate programs offered online:
Indiana University online programs are managed through the IU University-wide School of Continuing Studies which encompasses several IU campuses including Indiana University Purdue University Indianapolis (IUPUI), Indiana University Purdue University Fort Wayne (IPFW), and Indiana University East. Several programs are offered University-wide and made accessible through the Indiana University School of Continuing Studies (IU SCS).

AA – General Studies (IPFW) **
AA – General Studies (IUPUI)
AS – Histotechnology (IUPUI)
AS – Labor Studies (IU SCS)
BS – Business Administration (IU East) *
BA – Communication Studies (IU East) *
BGS – General Studies (IPFW) **
BGS – General Studies (IUPUI)
BS – Labor Studies (IU SCS)
BA – Technical & Professional Writing (IU East) *

*   Tuition for this program is (In state – $189.21 pch) (Out of state – $264.28 pch).

** Tuition for this program is (In state – $230.85 pch) (Out of state – $549.25 pch).

Fort Valley State University   (24)

1005 State University Drive
Fort Valley, GA 31030
(478) 825-6211
Website – www.fvsu.edu

Accreditation: Southern Association of Colleges and Schools.
www.sacs.org

Type of program offered online: Bachelor / Master
Programs accessible to students: Worldwide

Undergraduate tuition per credit hour online:
In state – $170.00
Out of state – $170.00

Undergraduate programs offered online:
BA – Criminal Justice
BA – Political Science
BA – Psychology
BA – Technical and Professional Writing

University of West Florida (25)

11000 University Parkway
Pensacola, FL 32514
(850) 474-2000
Website – www.uwf.edu

Accreditation: Southern Association of Colleges and Schools.
www.sacs.org

Type of program offered online: Certificate / Bachelor / Master
Programs accessible to students: Worldwide

Undergraduate tuition per credit hour online:
In state – $173.99 (With fee waiver)
Out of state – $173.99 (With fee waiver)

Undergraduate programs offered online:
BS – Career and Technical Studies
BS – Engineering Technology:
        Information Engineering Technology
BA – Exceptional Student Education
BS – Health Sciences
BS – Information Technology, Interdisciplinary:
        Networking and Telecommunications
BA – Maritime Studies
RN to BSN – Nursing
BS – Oceanography
Certificate – Arabic Language and Culture **
Certificate – Career and Technical Education
Certificate – Database Systems
Certificate – Geographic Information Science (GIS) *
Certificate – Human Performance Technology ***
Certificate – Medical Informatics
Certificate – Professional Accountancy
Certificate – Public Health
Certificate – Teacher Ready
Certificate – Technology Systems Support

*   Tuition per course for this program is $690.00 or ($230.00 pch).

**   Tuition per course for this program is $691.96 or ($230.65 pch).

*** Tuition per course for this program is $833.07 or ($277.69 pch).

Albany State University   (26)

504 College Drive
Albany, GA 31705
(229) 430-4600
Website – www.potentialrealized.org

Accreditation: Southern Association of Colleges and Schools.
www.sacs.org

Type of program offered online: Certificate / Bachelor / Master
Programs accessible to students: Worldwide

Undergraduate tuition per credit hour online:
In state – $175.00
Out of state – $175.00

Undergraduate programs offered online:
BS – Business Information Systems
Certificate – Biomedical Forensic Sciences *

*   Tuition per course for this program is $300.00 or ($100.00 pch).

Indiana University, East (27)

Whitewater Hall 151
2325 Chester Boulevard
Richmond, IN 47374-1289
(765) 973-8208
(800) 959-EAST (3278)
Website – www.iue.edu

Accreditation: North Central Association of Colleges and Schools. www.ncahlc.org

Type of program offered online: Certificate / Bachelor
Programs accessible to students: Worldwide

Undergraduate tuition per credit hour online:
In state – $180.54
Out of state – $254.36

Undergraduate programs offered online:
BS – Business Administration
BA – Communication Studies
BA – English:
    Technical and Professional Writing

Clear Creek Baptist College   (28)

300 Clear Creek Road
Pineville, KY 40977
(606) 337-3196
(866) 340-3196
Website – www.ccbbc.edu

Accreditation: Southern Association of Colleges and Schools.
www.sacs.org

Type of program offered online: Certificate / Associate /
Bachelor
Programs accessible to students: Worldwide

Undergraduate tuition per credit hour online:
In state – $182.00
Out of state – $182.00

Undergraduate programs offered online:
AA – Bi-Vocational Ministry
AA – Christian Service
AA – Pastoral Ministry
BA – Bi-Vocational Ministry
BA – Christian Service
BA – Pastoral Ministry

Emporia State University (29)

1200 Commercial Street
Emporia, KS 66801
(620) 341-1200
Website – www.emporia.edu

Accreditation: North Central Association of Colleges and Schools. www.ncahlc.org

Type of program offered online: Certificate / Bachelor / Master / Licensure
Programs accessible to students: Worldwide

Undergraduate tuition per credit hour online:
In state – $182.00
Out of state – $239.00

Undergraduate programs offered online:
BSB – Business
BSE – Elementary Education
BS – Information Resource Studies
BIS – Interdisciplinary Studies

University of Nebraska, Kearney (30)

905 West 25th Street
Kearney, NE 68849
(800) KEARNEY (532-7639)
Website – www.unk.edu

Accreditation: North Central Association of Colleges and Schools. www.ncahlc.org

Type of program offered online: Certificate / Bachelor / Master / Endorsement
Programs accessible to students: Worldwide

Undergraduate tuition per credit hour online:
In state – $184.00
Out of state – $284.25

Undergraduate programs offered online:
BS – Business Administration
BS – Organizational Communication
Endorsement – Vocational Diversified Occupations

Delta State University   (31)

Highway 8 West
Cleveland, MS 38733
(800) GO-TO-DSU (468-6378)
Website – www.deltastate.edu

Accreditation: Southern Association of Colleges and Schools.
www.sacs.org

Type of program offered online: Bachelor
Programs accessible to students: Worldwide

Undergraduate tuition per credit hour online:
In state – $185.00
Out of state – $466.00

Undergraduate programs offered online:
BBA – International Business & Development
RN to BSN – Nursing *

*   Residency requirement.

University of South Florida   (32)

4202 E. Fowler Avenue
Tampa, FL 33620
(813) 974-0405
Website – www.usf.edu

Accreditation: Southern Association of Colleges and Schools.
www.sacs.org

Type of program offered online: Certificate / Bachelor / Master
Programs accessible to students: Worldwide

Undergraduate tuition per credit hour online:
In state – $185.10
Out of state – $545.41

Undergraduate programs offered online:
BS – Applied Sciences:
        Criminal Justice
        Hospitality Management *
        Industrial Operations
        Information Technology
        Public Health
BA – Criminology *
BS – Nursing *

*   All required courses may not be available online.

Chadron State College (33)

1000 Main Street
Chadron, NE 69337
(800) CHADRON (242-3766)
Website – www.csc.edu

Accreditation: North Central Association of Colleges and Schools. www.ncahlc.org

Type of program offered online: Certificate / Bachelor / Master / Endorsement
Programs accessible to students: Worldwide

Undergraduate tuition per credit hour online:
In state – $190.00
Out of state – $190.00

Undergraduate programs offered online:
BA – Business Administration:
    Management
    Management Information Systems
    Marketing
BA – Family & Consumer Sciences:
    Child Development *
    Design & Merchandising *
    Human Services *
    Lifespan Wellness *
    Nutrition & Foods *
BA – General Business
BA – Interdisciplinary Studies
BA – Library Information Management
BS – Mathematics
BA – Psychology
BAS – Technical Occupations
Certificate – Family Life *
Certificate – Fashion *
Certificate – Hospitality *

Certificate – Parenting *
Certificate – Wellness *

*   All required courses may not be available online.

Peru State College (34)

P.O. Box 10
Peru, NE 68421
(800) 742-4412
Website – www.peru.edu

Accreditation: North Central Association of Colleges and Schools. www.ncahlc.org

Type of program offered online: Certificate / Bachelor / Master
Programs accessible to students: Worldwide

Undergraduate tuition per credit hour online:
In state – $190.00
Out of state – $190.00

Undergraduate programs offered online:
BAS – Applied Sciences:
    Management
BS – Business Administration:
    Accounting
    Computer & Management Information Systems
    Human Performance & Systems Management
    Marketing
BS – Criminal Justice:
    Administration
    Counseling
BS – Psychology

Southern Oregon University   (35)

1250 Siskiyou Boulevard
Ashland, OR 97520
(541) 552-7672
Website – www.sou.edu

Accreditation: Northwest Commission on Colleges and
Universities. www.nwccu.org

Type of program offered online: Certificate / Bachelor / Master
/ Licensure / Endorsement
Programs accessible to students: Worldwide

Undergraduate tuition per credit hour online:
In state – $190.00
Out of state – $190.00

Undergraduate programs offered online:
BBA – Business Administration:
    Accounting
    Management
    Management of Aging Services
BA – Criminology & Criminal Justice
BA/BS – Early Childhood Development
BAS – Management
Certificate – Accounting
Certificate – Non-Profit Management

University of Houston, Downtown (36)

One Main Street
Houston, TX 77002
(713) 221-8000
Website – www.uhd.edu

Accreditation: Southern Association of Colleges and Schools.
www.sacs.org

Type of program offered online: Bachelor
Programs accessible to students: Worldwide

Undergraduate tuition per credit hour online:
In state – $191.83
Out of state – $501.83

Undergraduate programs offered online:
BAAS – Criminal Justice
BS – Criminal Justice
BBA – General Business

Oregon Institute of Technology   (37)

3201 Campus Drive
Klamath Falls, OR 97601
(541) 885-1000
(800) 422-2017 ext. 1
Website – www.oit.edu

Accreditation: Northwest Commission on Colleges and Universities. www.nwccu.org

Type of program offered online: Certificate / Associate / Bachelor / Specialization / Minor
Programs accessible to students: Worldwide

Undergraduate tuition per credit hour online:
In state – $200.00
Out of state – $200.00

Undergraduate programs offered online:
AAS – Polysomnographic Technology
BS – Allied Health Management
BS – Dental Hygiene
BS – Echocardiography
BS – Information Technology
BS – Operations Management
BS – Radiologic Science
BS – Respiratory Care
BS – Vascular Technology
Minor – Applied Psychology
Minor – Business
Minor – Information Technology
Certificate – Polysomnographic Technology
Specialization – Picture Archiving & Communication Systems (PACS)

University of Northern Iowa   (38)

1227 West 27th Street
Cedar Falls, IA 50614
(319) 273-2311
Website – www.uni.edu

Accreditation: North Central Association of Colleges and Schools. www.ncahlc.org

Type of program offered online: Bachelor / Master / Doctorate
Programs accessible to students: Worldwide

Undergraduate tuition per credit hour online:
In state – $200.00
Out of state – $200.00

Undergraduate programs offered online:
BA – Elementary Education (2+2 Program) *
BLS – Liberal Studies
BA – Technology management (2+2 Program) *

*   Courses in this program are offered primarily via the Iowa Communications Network (ICN). Delivery of ICN Programs is limited to the state of Iowa.

Southern Polytechnic State University   (39)

1100 South Marietta Parkway
Marietta, GA 30060-2896
(678) 915-SPSU (7778)
(800) 635-3204
Website – www.spsu.edu

Accreditation: Southern Association of Colleges and Schools.
www.sacs.org

Type of program offered online: Certificate / Bachelor / Master
Programs accessible to students: Worldwide

Undergraduate tuition per credit hour online:
In state – $204.00
Out of state – $204.00

Undergraduate programs offered online:
BAS – Information Technology
BS – Information Technology (WebBSIT)
BAS – Manufacturing Operations
Certificate – Specialty Construction
Certificate – Technical Communication

Empire State College (40)

One Union Ave
Saratoga Springs, NY 12866
(518) 587-2100
Website – www.esc.edu

Accreditation: Middle States Association of Colleges and Schools. www.msche.org

Type of program offered online: Associate / Bachelor
Programs accessible to students: Worldwide

Undergraduate tuition per credit hour online:
In state – $207.00
Out of state – $207.00

Undergraduate programs offered online:
With the guidance of a faculty member, students will design a degree program utilizing courses and activities from the college's 11 broad areas of study listed below. From one of these areas of study, students will choose a concentration (similar to a major), other concentrations are possible however. Students can choose to earn an associate degree or extend their studies toward a bachelor degree.

– The Arts
– Business, Management & Economics
– Community and Human Services
– Cultural Studies
– Educational Studies
– Historical Studies
– Human Development
– Interdisciplinary Studies
– Labor Studies
– Science, Mathematics & Technology
– Social Theory, Social Structure and Change

Institute of Technology, Utica/Rome   (41)

100 Seymour Rd.
Utica, NY 13502
(315) 792-7500
Website – www.sunyit.edu

Accreditation: Middle States Association of Colleges and Schools. www.msche.org

Type of program offered online: Bachelor / Master
Programs accessible to students: Worldwide

Undergraduate tuition per credit hour online:
In state – $207.00
Out of state – $536.00

Undergraduate programs offered online:
BS – Health Information Management *
BS – Nursing *

* Residency requirement.

University of Maine, Augusta (42)

46 University Drive
Augusta, ME 04330-9410
(207) 621-3000
(877) UMA-1234 (862-1234)
Website – www.uma.edu

Accreditation: New England Association of Schools and Colleges. www.neasc.org

Type of program offered online: Associate / Bachelor
Programs accessible to students: Worldwide

Undergraduate tuition per credit hour online:
In state – $208.00
Out of state – $260.00

Undergraduate programs offered online:
AS – Business Administration
AA – Liberal Studies
AS – Library and Information Services
AS – Mental Health and Human Services
BAS – Applied Science
BS – Business Administration
BA – Liberal Studies
BS – Library and Information Services
BS – Mental Health and Human Services

Southeast Missouri State University   (43)

One University Plaza
Cape Girardeau, MO 63701
(573) 651-2766
Website – www.semo.edu

Accreditation: North Central Association of Colleges and Schools. www.ncahlc.org

Type of program offered online: Certificate / Bachelor / Master
Programs accessible to students: Worldwide

Undergraduate tuition per credit hour online:
In state – $208.50
Out of state – $363.00

Undergraduate programs offered online:
BS – Business Administration:
        Organizational Administration
BGS – General Studies
BS – Interdisciplinary Studies
RN to BSN – Nursing
BS – Technology Management

University of Maine, Fort Kent (44)

23 University Drive
Fort Kent, ME 04743
(207) 834-7500
(207) 834-7466 (TDD)
(888) TRY-UMFK (879-8635)
Website – www.umfk.maine.edu

Accreditation: New England Association of Schools and Colleges. www.neasc.org

Type of program offered online: Associate / Bachelor
Programs accessible to students: Worldwide

Undergraduate tuition per credit hour online:
In state – $211.00
Out of state – $531.00

Undergraduate programs offered online:
AA – Accounting
AA – Criminal Justice
AS – Information Assurance/Security
RN to BSN – Nursing
BS – Public Safety Administration
BUS – University Studies

State University of New York, Plattsburgh

101 Broad St.
Plattsburgh, NY 12901
(518) 564-2000
Website – www.plattsburgh.edu

Accreditation: Middle States Association of Colleges and Schools. www.msche.org

Type of program offered online: Bachelor
Programs accessible to students: Worldwide

Undergraduate tuition per credit hour online:
In state – $211.25
Out of state – $540.41

Undergraduate programs offered online:
RN to BSN – Nursing

Oklahoma Panhandle State University   (46)

P.O. Box 430
Goodwell, OK 73939
(580) 349-2611
(800) 664-OPSU (6778)
Website – www.opsu.edu

Accreditation: North Central Association of Colleges and Schools. www.ncahlc.org

Type of program offered online: Bachelor
Programs accessible to students: Worldwide

Undergraduate tuition per credit hour online:
In state – $212.66 *
Out of state – $212.66 *

Undergraduate programs offered online:
RN to BSN – Nursing

*   The per credit hour (pch) tuition rate is an estimate based on a student participating in two courses or 6 units. Please contact school for accurate account.

University of Hawaii, Hilo   (47)

200 W. Kawili St.
Hilo, HI 96720-4091
(808) 974-7414
(800) 897-4456
Website – www.uhh.hawaii.edu

Accreditation: Western Association of Schools and Colleges.
www.wascsenior.org

Type of program offered online: Certificate / Bachelor / Master
Programs accessible to students: Worldwide

Undergraduate tuition per credit hour online:
In state – $213.00
Out of state – $650.00

Undergraduate programs offered online:
RN to BSN – Nursing *
BA – Psychology *

*   Programs are currently only available to residents of Maui
       County, Kauai, and West Hawaii.

Valley City State University   (48)

101 College Street SW
Valley City, ND 58072
(800) 532-8641
Website – www.vcsu.edu

Accreditation: North Central Association of Colleges and
Schools. www.ncahlc.org

Type of program offered online: Certificate / Bachelor / Master
/ Endorsement / Minor
Programs accessible to students: Worldwide

Undergraduate tuition per credit hour online:
In state – $216.20
Out of state – $216.20

Undergraduate programs offered online:
BA/BS – Professional Communication
Minor – Library Media & Information Science
Minor – Teaching English Language Learners

Black Hills State University (49)

1200 University St.
Spearfish, SD 57799
(800) 255-2478
Website – www.bhsu.edu

Accreditation: North Central Association of Colleges and Schools. www.ncahlc.org

Type of program offered online: Bachelor / Master
Programs accessible to students: Worldwide

Undergraduate tuition per credit hour online:
In state – $217.70
Out of state – $267.10

Undergraduate programs offered online:
BS – Business Administration:
      Management

West Virginia University   (50)

P.O. Box 6201
Morgantown, WV 26506
(304) 293-0111
Website – www.wvu.edu

Accreditation: North Central Association of Colleges and Schools. www.ncahlc.org

Type of program offered online: Certificate / Bachelor / Master
Programs accessible to students: Worldwide

Undergraduate tuition per credit hour online:
In state – $222.00
Out of state – $705.00

Undergraduate programs offered online:
BA – Multidisciplinary Studies
RN to BSN – Nursing *
RBA – Regents Bachelor of Arts

*   Tuition for this program is (In state – $265.00 pch) (Out of state – $985.00 pch).

Midwestern State University (51)

3410 Taft Blvd.
Wichita Falls, TX 76308
(940) 397-4000
Website – www.mwsu.edu

Accreditation: Southern Association of Colleges and Schools.
www.sacs.org

Type of program offered online: Bachelor / Master
Programs accessible to students: Worldwide

Undergraduate tuition per credit hour online:
In state – $223.98
Out of state – $253.98

Undergraduate programs offered online:
BAAS – Applied Arts and Sciences
BS – Radiologic Science

Columbia College   (52)

1001 Rogers Street
Columbia, MO 65216
(573) 875-8700
(800) 231-2391
Website – www.ccis.edu

Accreditation: North Central Association of Colleges and
Schools. www.ncahlc.org

Type of program offered online: Associate / Bachelor / Master
Programs accessible to students: Worldwide

Undergraduate tuition per credit hour online:
In state – $225.00
Out of state – $225.00

Undergraduate programs offered online:
AS – Business Administration
AS – Criminal Justice Administration
AS – Environmental Studies
AS – Fire Service Administration *
AGS – General Studies
AS – Human Services
BA – American Studies
BA/BS – Business Administration
BA – Criminal Justice Administration
BGS – General Studies
BA – History
BA – Human Services
BA – Psychology
BA – Sociology

*   Available to Missouri residents only.

New Mexico State University (53)

P.O. Box 30001
Las Cruces, NM 88003-8001
(575) 646-0111
Website – www.nmsu.edu

Accreditation: North Central Association of Colleges and Schools. www.ncahlc.org

Type of program offered online: Certificate / Bachelor / Master / Doctorate / Licensure / Endorsement
Programs accessible to students: Worldwide

Undergraduate tuition per credit hour online:
In state – $225.00
Out of state – $225.00 *
$238.00 **
$695.00 ***

Undergraduate programs offered online:
BA – Sociology
BBA – General Business
BBA – Marketing
BCJ – Criminal Justice
BICT – Information and Communication Technology
BS – Hotel, Restaurant, and Tourism Management ****

* Non-resident students enrolling in 6 or less credit hours pay the NM resident rate.
** Non-resident students within a 135 mile radius of the New Mexico State University campus pay a tuition of ($238.00 pch).
*** Non-resident students enrolling in more than 6 credit hours pay ($695.00 pch).
**** Residency requirement.

Western Illinois University (54)

Sherman Hall / 1 University Circle
Macomb, IL 61455
(309) 298-1414
Website – www.wiu.edu

Accreditation: North Central Association of Colleges and Schools. www.ncahlc.org

Type of program offered online: Bachelor / Master
Programs accessible to students: Worldwide

Undergraduate tuition per credit hour online:
In state – $225.96 / $240.00 *
Out of state – $338.94 / $360.98 **

Undergraduate programs offered online:
BA – General Studies

* In state students as well as students from IA, IN, MO, and WI with an AA degree pay ($225.96 pch). Students without an AA degree pay ($240.00 pch).
** Out of state students excluding students from IA, IN, MO, and WI with an AA degree pay ($338.94 pch). Students without an AA degree pay ($360.98).

Utah State University   (55)

5055 Old Main Hill
Logan, UT 84322-5055
(435) 797-9700
(800) 233-2137
Website – www.usu.edu

Accreditation: Northwest Commission on Colleges and
Universities. www.nwccu.org

Type of program offered online: Certificate / Associate /
Bachelor / Master / Licensure / Minor
Programs accessible to students: Worldwide

Undergraduate tuition per credit hour online:
In state – $227.00
Out of state – $227.00

Undergraduate programs offered online:
AS – General Studies
BS – Agribusiness
BS – Communicative Disorders & Deaf Education
BS – Economics
BS – Family Life Studies
BS – Interdisciplinary Studies
BS – Psychology
Minor – Psychology
Minor – Spanish
Certificate – Deaf, Blindness
Certificate – Personal Financial Planning

State University of New York, (56)
College of Technology at Delhi

2 Main St.
Delhi, NY 13753
(800) 96-DELHI (963-3544)
Website – www.delhi.edu

Accreditation: Middle States Association of Colleges and Schools. www.msche.org

Type of program offered online: Associate / Bachelor
Programs accessible to students: Worldwide

Undergraduate tuition per credit hour online:
In state – $227.02
Out of state – $227.02

Undergraduate programs offered online:
AOS – Electrical Construction & Instrumentation
RN to BSN – Nursing
BBA – Veterinary Technology Management

Mississippi State University   (57)

P.O. Box 6334
Mississippi State, MS 39762
(662) 325-2323
Website – www.msstate.edu

Accreditation: Southern Association of Colleges and Schools.
www.sacs.org

Type of program offered online: Bachelor / Master / Doctorate
Programs accessible to students: Worldwide

Undergraduate tuition per credit hour online:
In state – $227.75
Out of state – $227.75

Undergraduate programs offered online:
BS – Elementary Education
BS – Geosciences:
      Broadcast Meteorology
      Operational Meteorology
BS – Interdisciplinary Studies

Boise State University (58)

1910 University Drive
Boise, ID 83725
(208) 426-1000
Website – www.boisestate.edu

Accreditation: Northwest Commission on Colleges and Universities. www.nwccu.org

Type of program offered online: Certificate / Bachelor / Master / Endorsement
Programs accessible to students: Worldwide

Undergraduate tuition per credit hour online:
In state – $232.00
Out of state – $316.00

Undergraduate programs offered online:
RN to BSN – Nursing
BS – Respiratory Care

Towson University (59)

8000 York Road
Towson, MD 21252-0001
(410) 704-2000
Website – www.towson.edu

Accreditation: Middle States Association of Colleges and Schools. www.msche.org

Type of program offered online: Bachelor
Programs accessible to students: Worldwide

Undergraduate tuition per credit hour online:
In state – $232.00
Out of state – $641.00

Undergraduate programs offered online:
BTPS – Allied Health:
      Administration & Management

Northwest Missouri State University   (60)

800 University Drive
Maryville, MO 64468
(660) 562-1212
Website – www.nwmissouri.edu

Accreditation: North Central Association of Colleges and
Schools. www.ncahlc.org

Type of program offered online: Certificate / Bachelor / Master
Programs accessible to students: Worldwide

Undergraduate tuition per credit hour online:
In state – $234.89
Out of state – $413.28

Undergraduate programs offered online:
BS – Business Management

Oregon State University   (61)

4943 The Valley Library
Corvallis, OR 97331-4504
(541) 737-2676
(800) 235-6559
Website – http://oregonstate.edu

Accreditation: Northwest Commission on Colleges and Universities. www.nwccu.org

Type of program offered online: Bachelor / Master / Minor
Programs accessible to students: Worldwide

Undergraduate tuition per credit hour online:
In state – $235.00
Out of state – $235.00

Undergraduate programs offered online:
BS – Environmental Sciences *
BS – Fisheries and Wildlife **
BS – General Agriculture **
BA/BS – General Anthropology
BS – General Horticulture **
BA/BS – Liberal Studies
BS – Natural Resources **
BA/BS – Political Science
BA/BS – Women Studies
Minor – Anthropolgy
Minor – Business & Entrepreneurship
Minor – Chemistry
Minor – Environmental Sciences
Minor – Fisheries and Wildlife
Minor – German
Minor – Natural Resources
Minor – Political Science
Minor – Psychology
Minor – Resource Economics

Minor – Sociology
Minor – U.S. History
Minor – Women Studies
Minor – Writing

* Not all courses are offered online.
** All course work except for the required year in lab biology are delivered online.

University of Maryland, University College

(62)

3501 University Blvd. East
Adelphia, MD 20783
(800) 888-UMUC (8682)
Website – www.umuc.edu

Accreditation: Middle States Association of Colleges and Schools. www.msche.org

Type of program offered online: Certificate / Bachelor / Master / Doctorate / Minor
Programs accessible to students: Worldwide

Undergraduate tuition per credit hour online:
In state – $237.00
Out of state – $499.00

Undergraduate programs offered online:
BS – Accounting
BA – Asian Studies
BS – Business Administration
BA – Communication Studies
BS – Computer & Information Science
BS – Computer Information Technology
BS – Computer Science
BS – Computer Studies
BS – Criminal Justice
BS – Cybersecurity
BS – Emergency Management
BA – English
BS – Environmental Management
BS – Finance
BS – Fire Science
BS – Gerontology
BS – Global Business & Public Policy
BA – History

BS – Homeland Security
BA – Humanities
BS – Human Resource Management
BS – Information Systems Management
BS – Investigative Forensics
BS – Legal Studies
BS – Management Studies
BS – Marketing
BS – Political Science
BS – Psychology
BS – Social Science
Minor – Accounting
Minor – African American Studies
Minor – Asian Studies
Minor – Biology
Minor – Business Administration
Minor – Business Law & Public Policy
Minor – Business Supply Chain Management
Minor – Communication Studies
Minor – Computing
Minor – Criminal Justice
Minor – Customer Service Management
Minor – Economics
Minor – Emergency Management
Minor – English
Minor – Environmental Management
Minor – Finance
Minor – Fire Science
Minor – Forensics
Minor – Gerontology
Minor – History
Minor – Homeland Security
Minor – Humanities
Minor – Human Resource Management
Minor – International Business Management
Minor – Journalism
Minor – Marketing

Minor – Natural Science
Minor – Philosophy
Minor – Political Science
Minor – Psychology
Minor – Sociology
Minor – Speech Communication
Minor – Strategic & Entrepreneurial Management
Minor – Women's Studies
Certificate – Accounting-Introductory
Certificate – Accounting-Advanced
Certificate – Applied Behavioral Social Sciences
Certificate – Business Project Management
Certificate – Clinical Mental Health Care
Certificate – Computer Networking
Certificate – Database Design & Implementation
Certificate – Database Management
Certificate – Financial Management
Certificate – Health Issues for the Aging Adult
Certificate – Human Resource Management
Certificate – Information Assurance
Certificate – Information Management
Certificate – Internet Technologies
Certificate – Management Foundations
Certificate – Object Oriented Design & Programming
Certificate – Paralegal Studies
Certificate – Project Management for IT Professionals
Certificate – Visual Basic Programming
Certificate – Workplace Communications
Certificate – Workplace Spanish

Minot State University (63)

500 University Avenue West
Minot, ND 58707
(800) 777-0750
Website – www.minotstateu.edu

Accreditation: North Central Association of Colleges and Schools. www.ncahlc.org

Type of program offered online: Certificate / Associate / Bachelor / Master
Programs accessible to students: Worldwide

Undergraduate tuition per credit hour online:
In state – $239.63
Out of state – $239.63

Undergraduate programs offered online:
AS – Developmental Disabilities
BAS – Applied Business Information Technology
BAS – Applied Management
BGS – General Studies
BS – International Business
BS – Management
BS – Management Information Systems
BS – Marketing
BS – Nursing for Registered Nurses
Certificate – Application Software Specialist
Certificate – Developmental Disabilities
Certificate – Web Development

Western Governors University   (64)

4001 South 700 East, Suite 700
Salt Lake City, UT 84107-2533
(801) 274-3280
Website – www.wgu.edu

Accreditation: Northwest Commission on Colleges and
Universities. www.nwccu.org

Type of program offered online: Bachelor / Master / Licensure
Programs accessible to students: Worldwide

Undergraduate tuition per credit hour online:
In state – $240.83
Out of state – $240.83

Undergraduate programs offered online:
WGU treats all students as "full-time" and charges tuition at
a flat rate regardless of the number of credit hours attempted
or completed. The "standard term" is based upon a full-time
enrollment of at least 12 credit hours for undergraduate students and 8 credit hours for graduate students. Students who
complete more or fewer units are charged the same tuition rate.
The per credit hour tuition rate posted above is based on a
full-time undergraduate enrollment of 12 hours at a flat rate of
($2,890.00).

BS – Accounting
BS – Business:
      Human Resource Management
      Information Technology Management
BS – Business Management
BA – Early Childhood Education
BS – Health Informatics
BS – Information Technology:
      Databases
      Networks Administration

Networks Design & Management
Security
Software
BA – Interdisciplinary Studies (K-8)
BS – Marketing Management
BA – Mathematics (5-9 or 5-12)
RN to BSN – Nursing *
BS – Nursing (Prelincensure) **
BS – Sales & Sales Management
BA – Science (5-9)
BA – Science:
Biological Sciences (5-12)
Chemistry (5-12)
Geosciences (5-12)
Physics (5-12)
BA – Special Education (K-12)

*   Flat rate tuition is ($3,250.00) or ($270.83 pch). (This is an estimate of the cost per credit hour, please contact school for accurate account).

** Flat rate tuition is (4,250.00) or ($354.16 pch). (This is an estimate of the cost per credit hour, please contact school for accurate account).

Ball State University   (65)

2000 W. University Ave
Muncie, IN 47306
(765) 289-1241
(800) 382-8540
Website – cms.bsu.edu

Accreditation: North Central Association of Colleges and Schools. www.ncahlc.org

Type of program offered online: Certificate / Associate / Bachelor / Master / Doctorate / Specialist
/ Licensure
Programs accessible to students: Worldwide

Undergraduate tuition per credit hour online:
In state – $244.00
Out of state – $434.00

Undergraduate programs offered online:
AA – General Arts
AS – Business Administration:
        Management
BGS – General Studies
RN to BSN – Nursing
Certificate – Corrections
Certificate – Emerging Media Journalism
Certificate – Web Applications

American Public University System   (66)

111 W. Congress Street
Charles Town, WV 25414
(877) 755-2787
Website – www.apus.edu

Accreditation: North Central Association of Colleges and Schools. www.ncahlc.org

Type of program offered online: Certificate / Associate / Bachelor / Master
Programs accessible to students: Worldwide

Undergraduate tuition per credit hour:
In state – $250.00
Out of state – $250.00

Undergraduate programs offered online:
AA – Accounting
AA – Business Administration
AA – Communication
AS – Computer Applications
AA – Counter Terrorism Studies
AS – Database Application Development
AA – Early Childhood Care & Education
AS – Explosive Ordinance Disposal
AS – Fire Science
AA – General Studies
AA – History
AA – Hospitality
AA – Management
AA – Military History
AS – Paralegal Studies
AS – Public Health
AA – Real Estate Studies
AA – Weapons of Mass Destruction Preparedness
AS – Web Publishing

BBA – Business Administration
BA – Child & Family Development
BA/BS – Criminal Justice
BA – Emergency and Disaster Management
BA – English
BS – Environmental Studies
BS – Fire Science Management
BA – General Studies
BA – History
BA – Homeland Security
BA – Hospitality Management
BS – Information Systems Security
BS – Information Technology
BS – Information Technology Management
BA – Intelligence Studies
BA – International Relations
BS – Legal Studies
BA – Management
BA – Marketing
BA – Middle Eastern Studies
BA – Military History
BA – Military Management & Program Acquisition
BA – Philosophy
BA – Political Science
BA – Psychology
BS – Public Health
BA – Religion
BA – Security Management
BA – Sociology
BS – Space Studies
BS – Sports & Health Sciences
BA – Transportation & Logistics Management
Certificate – Computer Systems & Networks
Certificate – Corrections Management
Certificate – Cybercrime Essentials
Certificate – Enterprise Web Applications
Certificate – Enterprise Web Applications Using .Net

Certificate – Explosive Ordnance Disposal
Certificate – Family Studies
Certificate – Fire Science
Certificate – Forensics
Certificate – Hazardous Waste Management
Certificate – Homeland Security
Certificate – Human Resource Management
Certificate – Infant & Toddler Care
Certificate – Information Security Planning
Certificate – Information Systems Security Essentials
Certificate – Instructional Design & Delivery
Certificate – Intelligence Analysis
Certificate – Internet Webmaster
Certificate – IT Infrastructure Security
Certificate – IT Project Management Essentials
Certificate – Microsoft Access Database Applications
Certificate – Microsoft Office Applications
Certificate – Military Leadership Studies
Certificate – Paralegal Studies
Certificate – Real Estate Management
Certificate – Security Management
Certificate – Space Studies
Certificate – Terrorism Studies
Certificate – United Nations
Certificate – Visual Basic Application Development
Certificate – Visual Communications
Certificate – Weapons of Mass Destruction Preparedness
Certificate – Web Publishing
Certificate – Web 2.0

Toccoa Falls College (67)

107 N. Chapel Dr.
Toccoa Falls, GA 30598
(706) 886-6831
(888) 785-5624
Website – www.tfc.edu

Accreditation: Southern Association of Colleges and Schools.
www.sacs.org

Type of program offered online: Certificate / Bachelor
Programs accessible to students: Worldwide

Undergraduate tuition per credit hour:
In state – $250.00
Out of state – $250.00

Undergraduate programs offered online:
BS – Ministry Leadership
BBA – Non-Profit Business Administration

Troy University (68)

Troy University Extended Learning Center
1101 S. Brundidge Street
Troy, AL 36082
(334) 670-5876
(800) 414-5756
Website – www.troy.edu

Accreditation: Southern Association of Colleges and Schools.
www.sacs.org

Type of program offered online: Associate / Bachelor / Master
Programs accessible to students: Worldwide

Undergraduate tuition per credit hour online:
In state – $250.00
Out of state – $250.00

Undergraduate programs offered online:
AS – Business
AS – General Education
BS – Applied Computer Science
BS – Business Administration:
    General Business
    Management
BS – Criminal Justice
BS – History
BS – Interpreter Training
BS – Political Science
BS – Psychology
BAS – Resource & Technology Management
BS – Social Science
BS – Sport & Fitness Management

University of Northwestern Ohio   (69)

1441 N. Cable Rd.
Lima, OH 45805
(419) 998-3120
Website – www.unoh.edu

Accreditation: North Central Association of Colleges and Schools. www.ncahlc.org

Type of program offered online: Diploma / Associate / Bachelor
Programs accessible to students: Worldwide

Undergraduate tuition per credit hour online:
In state – $250.00
Out of state – $250.00

Undergraduate programs offered online:
AA – Accounting
AA – Agribusiness Marketing / Management Technology
AA – Business Administration
AA – Legal Assisting
AA – Legal Office Management
AA – Marketing
AA – Medical Office Management
AA – Office Management
AA – Specialized Studies
AA – Travel & Hotel Management
AA – Word Processing / Administrative Support
BA – Accounting
BA – Accounting (CPA Track)
BA – Business Administration
BA – Business Administration:
     Agribusiness Management
     Marketing
BA – Forensic Accounting
BA – Health Care Administration

BA – Marketing
BA – Specialized Studies
Diploma – Agribusiness Management
Diploma – Executive Assistant
Diploma – Medical Coding
Diploma – Medical Transcriptionist
Diploma – Paralegal
Diploma – Travel & Hospitality
Diploma – Word Processing Specialist

University of Nebraska, Lincoln   (70)

1400 R Street
Lincoln, NE 68588
(402) 472-7211
Website – www.unl.edu

Accreditation: North Central Association of Colleges and Schools. www.ncahlc.org

Type of program offered online: Certificate / Bachelor
Programs accessible to students: Worldwide

Undergraduate tuition per credit hour online:
In state – $251.10
Out of state – $422.82

Undergraduate programs offered online:
BS – Applied Science:
        Agricultural Systems
        Integrative Systems
Certificate – Agriculture & Natural Resources Legal Studies
Certificate – Meat Culinology
Certificate – Public Policy

Dickinson State University (71)

291 Campus Drive
Dickinson, ND 58601
(701) 483-2507
(800) 279-HAWK (4295)
Website – www.dickinsonstate.edu

Accreditation: North Central Association of Colleges and Schools. www.ncahlc.org

Type of program offered online: Associate / Bachelor
Programs accessible to students: Worldwide

Undergraduate tuition per credit hour online:
In state – $252.00
Out of state – $252.00

Undergraduate programs offered online:
AS – Agriculture Sales and Service Equine Management
AA – General Studies
BS – Business Administration
BS – Finance
BS – Human Resource Management
BS – International Business
BAS – Technology
BUS – University Studies

Minnesota State University, Moorhead   (72)

1104 7th Avenue South
Moorhead, MN 56563
(800) 593-7246
Website – www.mnstate.edu

Accreditation: North Central Association of Colleges and Schools. www.ncahlc.org

Type of program offered online: Certificate / Bachelor / Master / Licensure
Programs accessible to students: Worldwide

Undergraduate tuition per credit hour online:
In state – $253.53
Out of state – $253.53

Undergraduate programs offered online:
RN to BSN – Nursing
BS – Operations Management
Certificate – Teaching and Learning with Technology *

*   Residency requirement.

Bemidji State University (73)

1500 Birchmont Drive NE
Bemidji, MN 56601-2699
(218) 755-2001
(800) 475-2001
Website – www.bemidjistate.edu

Accreditation: North Central Association of Colleges and Schools. www.ncahlc.org

Type of program offered online: Bachelor / Master
Programs accessible to students: Worldwide

Undergraduate tuition per credit hour online:
In state – $256.43
Out of state – $256.43

Undergraduate programs offered online:
BAS – Applied Engineering *
BS – Business Administration
BS – Criminal Justice
RN to BSN – Nursing *
BS – Teacher Education (DLiTE Program) *
BAS – Technology Management *

* Residency requirement.

Old Dominion University   (74)

Office of Admissions
108 Alfred B. Rollins Jr. Hall
Norfolk, VA 23529-0050
(757) 683-3685
(800) 348-7926
Website – www.odu.edu

Accreditation: Southern Association of Colleges and Schools.
www.sacs.org

Type of program offered online: Certificate / Bachelor / Master
/ Minor
Programs accessible to students: Worldwide

Undergraduate tuition per credit hour online:
In state – $258.00
Out of state – $706.00

Undergraduate programs offered online:
BS – Criminal Justice
BSDH – Dental Hygiene
RN to BSN – Nursing
Minor – Criminal Justice
Minor – Training & Development

Dakota State University (75)

820 N. Washington Ave
Madison, SD 57042
(605) 256-5111
(888) DSU-9988 (378-9988)
Website – www.dsu.edu

Accreditation: North Central Association of Colleges and Schools. www.ncahlc.org

Type of program offered online: Certificate / Associate / Bachelor / Master / Doctorate/ Minor
Programs accessible to students: Worldwide

Undergraduate tuition per credit hour online:
In state – $258.80
Out of state – $258.80

Undergraduate programs offered online:
AS – Application Programming
AS – Business Management
AA – General Studies
AS – Health Information Technology
BS – Computer Information Systems
BS – Health Information Administration
BBA – Management Information Systems
Minor – Computer & Network Security
Minor – Professional & Technical Communication
Certificate – Healthcare Coding

Northern State University (76)

1200 South Jay Street
Aberdeen, SD 57401
(800) NSU-5330 (678-5330)
Website – www.northern.edu

Accreditation: North Central Association of Colleges and Schools. www.ncahlc.org

Type of program offered online: Certificate / Associate / Bachelor
Programs accessible to students: Worldwide

Undergraduate tuition per credit hour online:
In state – $258.80
Out of state – $258.80

Undergraduate programs offered online:
AS – Paraprofessional Education *
BS – Accounting **
BS – Banking & Financial Services ****
BS – Business Administration **
BS – Finance **
BA – International Business Studies **
BS – Marketing **
BS – Professional Accountancy ***
BA – Speech Communication ***
Certificate – Executive Banking

*   This proposed online degree is currently in development with an anticipated completion date of Spring 2011.
**   This proposed online degree is currently in development with an anticipated completion date of Fall 2011.
***   This proposed online degree is currently in development with an anticipated completion date of Spring 2012
**** This proposed online degree is currently in development with an anticipated completion date of Fall 2012.

South Dakota State University (77)

Admissions Office
Box 2201
Brookings, SD 57007
(800) 952-3541
Website – www.sdstate.edu

Accreditation: North Central Association of Colleges and Schools. www.ncahlc.org

Type of program offered online: Associate / Bachelor / Master
Programs accessible to students: Worldwide

Undergraduate tuition per credit hour online:
In state – $258.80
Out of state – $258.80

Undergraduate programs offered online:
AA – General Studies
BS – Interdisciplinary Studies
BS – Interdisciplinary Studies:
     Social Sciences
RN to BSN – Nursing

University of South Dakota   (78)

414 E. Clark St.
Vermillion, SD 57069
(877) COYOTES (269-6837)
Website – www.usd.edu

Accreditation: North Central Association of Colleges and Schools. www.ncahlc.org

Type of program offered online: Certificate / Associate / Bachelor / Master / Doctorate / Specialist
Programs accessible to students: Worldwide

Undergraduate tuition per credit hour online:
In state – $258.80
Out of state – $258.80

Undergraduate programs offered online:
AA – General Studies
AS – Nursing *
BS – Alcohol & Drug Studies
BGS – General Studies
BS – Health Sciences
Certificate – Alcohol & Drug Studies

*   This program is only available to employees of The Evangelical Lutheran Good Samaritan Society ("GSS" or "The Society").

Granite State College (79)

Old Suncook Road
Concord, NH 03301
(603) 228-3000
(888) 228-3000
Website – www.granite.edu

Accreditation: New England Association of Schools and Colleges. www.neasc.org

Type of program offered online: Associate / Bachelor
Programs accessible to students: Worldwide

Undergraduate tuition per credit hour online:
In state – $260.00
Out of state – $275.00

Undergraduate programs offered online:
AS – Behavioral Science
AS – Business
AS – Early Childhood Education
AA – General Studies
BS – Applied Studies
BS – Behavioral Science
BS – Business Management
BS – Criminal Justice
BS – Criminal Justice:
     Criminal Justice Administration
BS – Early Childhood Education
BA/BS – Individualized Studies

Drury University   (80)

900 North Benton Avenue
Springfield, MO 65802
(417) 873-7879
(800) 922-2274
Website – www.drury.edu

Accreditation: North Central Association of Colleges and
Schools. www.ncahlc.org

Type of program offered online: Certificate / Associate /
Bachelor / Master
Programs accessible to students: Worldwide

Undergraduate tuition per credit hour online:
In state – $261.00
Out of state – $261.00

Undergraduate programs offered online:
AS – Business Administration
AS – Criminal Justice
AS – English
AS – Environmental Management
AS – General Studies
AS – Law Enforcement
AS – Organizational Studies
AS – Paralegal Studies
AS – Psychology
BBA – Business Administration
BS – Criminal Justice
BS – General Studies
BS – Health Services
BS – History
BS – Human Services
BS – Instructional Technology

BS – Law Enforcement
BS – Organizational Studies
BS – Psychology
BS – Sociology

Colorado Technical University   (81)

4435 North Chestnut Street
Colorado Springs, CO 80907
(866) 942-6555
Website – www.coloradotech.edu

Accreditation: North Central Association of Colleges and Schools. www.ncahlc.org

Type of program offered online: Associate / Bachelor / Master
Programs accessible to students: Worldwide

Undergraduate tuition per credit hour online:
In state – $265.00
Out of state – $265.00

Undergraduate programs offered online:
AS – Accounting
AS – Business Administration
AS – Criminal Justice
AS – General Studies
AS – Health Administrative Services
AS – Medical Billing & Coding
BS – Accounting *
BS – Business Administration: *
     Finance *
     Healthcare Management *
     Human Resource Management *
     Information Technology *
     International Business *
     Management *
     Marketing *
     Project Management *
     Property Management *
BS – Criminal Justice *
BS – Criminal Justice: *

Homeland Security and Emergency Management *
Human Services *
BS – Financial Forensics *
BS – Financial Planning *
BS – Health Services Administration *
BS – Information Technology: *
Network Management *
Security *
Software Application Programming *
Software Systems Engineering *
Web Development *
BS – Management *
BS – Nursing *
BS – Technology Management *

*   Tuition for this program is (In state / Out of state – $340.00 pch).

Mayville State University   (82)

330 Third Street NE
Mayville, ND 58257
(800) 437-4104
Website – www.mayvillestate.edu

Accreditation: North Central Association of Colleges and Schools. www.ncahlc.org

Type of program offered online: Associate / Bachelor
Programs accessible to students: Worldwide

Undergraduate tuition per credit hour online:
In state – $265.00
Out of state – $265.00

Undergraduate programs offered online:
AA – Early Childhood *
BS – Business Administration *
BAS – Business Administration
BA – Early Childhood *
BS – Education: *
      Early Childhood Education *
      Elementary Education *

*   Residency requirement.

Metropolitan State University (83)

700 East Seventh Street
Saint Paul, MN 55106
(651) 793-1300
Website – www.metrostate.edu

Accreditation: North Central Association of Colleges and Schools. www.ncahlc.org

Type of program offered online: Certificate / Bachelor / Master / Doctorate
Programs accessible to students: Worldwide

Undergraduate tuition per credit hour online:
In state – $265.88
Out of state – $265.88

Undergraduate programs offered online:
BS – Business Administration
BS – Finance
BS – Human Resource Management
BS – Individualized Studies
BS – Industrial Management
BS – Law Enforcement (For licensed Police Officers) *
BS – Management
BS – Marketing
BAS – Organizational Administration
Certificate – Wound, Ostomy, and Continence (WOC) Program **

* Residency requirement.
** Tuition for this program is (In state / Out of state – $506.78 pch).

Austin Peay State University   (84)

601 College Street
Clarksville, TN 37044
(931) 221-7011
(877) 861-APSU (861-2778)
Website – www.apsu.edu

Accreditation: Southern Association of Colleges and Schools.
www.sacs.org

Type of program offered online: Bachelor
Programs accessible to students: Worldwide

Undergraduate tuition per credit hour online:
In state – $267.00
Out of state – $764.00

Undergraduate programs offered online:
BS – Computer Science & Information Systems
BPS – Professional Studies

North Dakota State University   (85)

1340 Administration Avenue
Fargo, ND 58102
(701) 231-8011
Website – www.ndsu.edu

Accreditation: North Central Association of Colleges and Schools. www.ncahlc.org

Type of program offered online: Certificate / Bachelor / Master / Endorsement
Programs accessible to students: Worldwide

Undergraduate tuition per credit hour online:
In state – $267.11
Out of state – $267.11

Undergraduate programs offered online:
BS – Human Development & Family Science:
    Child Development
    Family Science
LPN to BSN – Nursing *
RN to BSN – Nursing *
BA/BS – Sociology
BUS – University Studies
Minor – Human Development & Family Science **
Minor – Psychology **
Minor – Sociology **

*   Residency requirement.
** This minor is available to NDSU students completing a bachelor's degree.

University of Central Missouri (86)

P.O. Box 800
Warrensburg, MO 64093
(877) 729-8266
Website – www.ucmo.edu

Accreditation: North Central Association of Colleges and Schools. www.ncahlc.org

Type of program offered online: Certificate / Bachelor / Master / Minor
Programs accessible to students: Worldwide

Undergraduate tuition per credit hour online:
In state – $267.30
Out of state – $267.30

Undergraduate programs offered online:
BS – Criminal Justice
BS – Crisis & Disaster Management
RN to BSN – Nursing
BS – Occupational Education
Minor – Child & Family Development
Minor – Psychology
Minor – Religious Studies

Ohio Christian University (87)

1476 Lancaster Pike
Circleville, OH 43113
(877) 762-8669
Website – www.ohiochristian.edu

Accreditation: North Central Association of Colleges and Schools. www.ncahlc.org

Type of program offered online: Certificate / Associate / Bachelor
Programs accessible to students: Worldwide

Undergraduate tuition per credit hour online:
In state – $270.00
Out of state – $270.00
Military – $250.00

Undergraduate programs offered online:
AA – Business:
    Agribusiness
AA – Business Management
AA – Christian Ministry
AA – Interdisciplinary Studies
BA – Business: *
    Business Management *
    Healthcare Management *
    Logistics Management *
BA – Interdisciplinary Studies *
BA – Practical Leadership *
BA – Psychology *
BA – Substance Abuse Counseling *

* Tuition for this program is (In state / Out of state – $395.00 pch) excluding military personnel who are given a rate of ($250.00 pch) for all programs.

Indiana State University   (88)

200 North Seventh Street
Terre Haute, IN 47809
(812) 237-6311
(800) GO TO ISU (468-6478)
Website – www.indstate.edu

Accreditation: North Central Association of Colleges and Schools. www.ncahlc.org

Type of program offered online: Certificate / Bachelor / Master / Doctorate / Licensure
Programs accessible to students: Worldwide

Undergraduate tuition per credit hour online:
In state – $272.00
Out of state – $340.00

Undergraduate programs offered online:
BS – Adult and Career Education
BS – Business Administration
BA/BS – Criminology and Criminal Justice
BS – Electronics Engineering Technology
BS – Human Resource Development
BS – Insurance and Risk Management
BS – Mechanical Engineering Technology
LPN/LVN to BSN – Nursing
RN to BSN – Nursing
BS – Technology Management
Minor – Accounting
Minor – Forensic Accounting
Minor – Human Resource Development
Minor – Packaging *
Certificate – Criminology:
                Corrections
                Law Enforcement
                Private Security and Loss Prevention

Certificate – Driver Education *
Certificate – Post-Secondary Facilitator

*   Residency requirement

Nichols College   (89)

124 Center Road
Dudley, MA 01571
(508) 213-1560
(800) 470-3379
Website – www.nichols.edu

Accreditation: New England Association of Schools and
Colleges. www.neasc.org

Type of program offered online: Certificate / Bachelor / Master
Programs accessible to students: Worldwide

Undergraduate tuition per credit hour online:
In state – $275.00
Out of state – $275.00

Undergraduate programs offered online:
BA/BS – Criminal Justice Management
BA/BS – Finance
BA/BS – General Business
BA/BS – Marketing
BA – Psychology

Saint Joseph's College, Maine (90)

278 White's Bridge Road
Standish, MN 04084
(800) 752-4723
Website – www.sjcme.edu

Accreditation: New England Association of Schools and Colleges. www.neasc.org

Type of program offered online: Certificate / Associate / Bachelor / Master
Programs accessible to students: Worldwide

Undergraduate tuition per credit hour online:
In state – $275.00
Out of state – $275.00

Undergraduate programs offered online:
AS – Adult Education & Training
AS – Business Administration
AS – Criminal Justice
AS – General Studies:
    Human Services
    Psychology
AS – Radiologic Science Administration **
BS – Business Administration
BS – General Studies:
    Adult Education & Training
    Business Administration
    Criminal Justice
    Human Services
    Psychology
BS – Health Administration **
BS – Long Term Care Administration **
RN to BSN – Nursing **
BS – Radiologic Science Administration **
BA – Theological Studies *

Certificate – Adult Education & Training
Certificate – Health Care Management **
Certificate – Long Term Care Administration **

*   Tuition for this program is (In state / Out of state – $280.00 pch).

**   Tuition for this program is (In state / Out of state – $325.00 pch).

Taylor University   (91)

236 West Reade Ave
Upland, IN 46989
(800) 882-3456
Website – www.taylor.edu

Accreditation: North Central Association of Colleges and
Schools. www.ncahlc.org

Type of program offered online: Associate / Bachelor
Programs accessible to students: Worldwide

Undergraduate tuition per credit hour online:
In state – $275.00
Out of state – $275.00

Undergraduate programs offered online:
AA – Biblical Studies
AA – Justice Administration:
　　　Ministry
　　　Public Policy
　　　Social Work
AA – Liberal Arts:
　　　Business
　　　Christian Ministries
　　　Discipleship
　　　History
　　　Professional Writing
　　　Social Science
BBA – Business Administration *

*　Tuition for major courses in this program is ($350.00 pch).

University of Wisconsin, Superior (92)

Belknap & Catlin
P.O. Box 2000
Superior, WI 54880
(715) 394-8101
Website – www.uwsuper.edu

Accreditation: North Central Association of Colleges and Schools. www.ncahlc.org

Type of program offered online: Bachelor
Programs accessible to students: Worldwide

Undergraduate tuition per credit hour online:
In state – $275.00
Out of state – $275.00

Undergraduate programs offered online:
BA – Communicating Arts
BA – Elementary Education
BA – Individually Designed
BA – Sustainable Management

Minors for Communicating Arts Majors
– Geography
– Health
– Health and Human Performance
– Individually Designed
– Library Science
– Philosophy
– Psychology

Minors for Elementary Education Majors
– Adaptive Education / Special Education
– Broadfield Language Arts / Reading Teaching
– Early Childhood
– Geography EC-EA

- Health Education EC-A
- Health Education MC-EA
- Library Science EC-A
- Social Studies Teaching

Minors for Individually Designed Majors
- Geography
- Health
- Health and Human Performance
- Library Science
- Philosophy
- Professional and Personal Communication
- Psychology

Norfolk State University (93)

700 Park Avenue
Norfolk, VA 23504
(757) 823-8600
Website – www.nsu.edu

Accreditation: Southern Association of Colleges and Schools.
www.sacs.org

Type of program offered online: Bachelor
Programs accessible to students: Worldwide

Undergraduate tuition per credit hour online:
In state – $275.39
Out of state – $710.50

Undergraduate programs offered online:
BS – Interdisciplinary Studies

Saint Cloud State University   (94)

720 4th Avenue South
St. Cloud, MN 56301-4498
(320) 308-0121
Website – www.stcloudstate.edu

Accreditation: North Central Association of Colleges and Schools. www.ncahlc.org

Type of program offered online: Bachelor / Master / Minor / Licensure
Programs accessible to students: Worldwide

Undergraduate tuition per credit hour:
In state – $275.75
Out of state – $275.75

Undergraduate programs offered online:
BES – Community Psychology
BA – Criminal Justice Studies
Minor – Community Psychology
Minor – Criminal Justice Studies
Minor – Psychology
Licensure – Driver Education Teacher Preparation

Wayland Baptist University (95)

1900 W. 7th Street
Plainview, TX 79072
(806) 291-1000
(800) 588-1928
Website – www.wbu.edu

Accreditation: Southern Association of Colleges and Schools.
www.sacs.org

Type of program offered online: Associate / Bachelor / Master
Programs accessible to students: Worldwide

Undergraduate tuition per credit hour online:
In state – $276.00
Out of state – $276.00

Undergraduate programs offered online:
AAS – Applied Science *
BAS – Applied Science
BCM – Christian Ministry
BS – Nursing

* Residency requirement

Jacksonville State University (96)

700 Pelham Road North
Jacksonville, AL 36265-1602
(800) 231-JAX1 (5291)
Website – www.jsu.edu

Accreditation: Southern Association of Colleges and Schools.
www.sacs.org

Type of program offered online: Certificate / Bachelor / Master / Minor
Programs accessible to students: Worldwide

Undergraduate tuition per credit hour online:
In state – $280.00
Out of state – $280.00

Undergraduate programs offered online:
BS – Business / Management
BS – Emergency Management with a Minor in Homeland
    Security
BS – Emergency Management with a Minor in Public Safety
    Telecommunications
BS – Family & Consumer Sciences:
    Child Development
RN to BSN – Nursing (STEP Program)

United States Sports Academy (97)

One Academy Drive
Daphne, AL 36526
(251) 626-3303
(800) 223-2668
Website – www.ussa.edu

Accreditation: Southern Association of Colleges and Schools.
www.sacs.org

Type of program offered online: Certificate / Bachelor / Master
/ Certification / Diploma
Programs accessible to students: Worldwide

Undergraduate tuition per credit hour online:
In state – $280.00
Out of state – $280.00
Military – $250.00 (200-400 level courses)

Undergraduate programs offered online:
BSS – Sports Science

University of Illinois, Springfield   (98)

One University Plaza
Springfield, IL 62703
(217) 206-6600
Website – www.uis.edu

Accreditation: North Central Association of Colleges and
Schools. www.ncahlc.org

Type of program offered online: Certificate / Bachelor / Master
/ Minor
Programs accessible to students: Worldwide

Undergraduate tuition per credit hour online:
In state – $282.50
Out of state – $282.50

Undergraduate programs offered online:
BBA – Business Administration
BS – Computer Science
BA – English
BA – History
BA – Liberal Studies
BA – Mathematics
BA – Philosophy
Minor – Mathematics
Minor – Philosophy
Minor – Women & Gender Studies

Wheeling Jesuit University   (99)

316 Washington Avenue
Wheeling, WV 26003
(800) 624-6992
Website – www.wju.edu

Accreditation: North Central Association of Colleges and
Schools. www.ncahlc.org

Type of program offered online: Certificate / Bachelor / Master
Programs accessible to students: Worldwide

Undergraduate tuition per credit hour online:
In state – $285.00
Out of state – $285.00

Undergraduate programs offered online:
RN to BSN – Nursing
RN to MSN – Nursing: *
                Family Nurse Practitioner *
                Nursing Administration *
                Nursing Education Specialist *
Certificate – (ACT) Accelerated Certification for Teaching **

NOTE: Clinical courses for the nursing programs listed above
          are not available online. Clinical experiences usually
          occur in the student's home community.

*   At the completion of this online program, the graduate
    achieves both the BSN degree and the MSN degree. Tuition
    for MSN courses is (In state / Out of state – $500.00 pch).
** Tuition for this program is (In state / Out of state – $375.00
    pch).

Colorado State University (100)

Office of Admissions
1062 Campus Delivery
Fort Collins, CO 80523-1062
(970) 491-6909
(877) 491-4336
Website – www.colostate.edu

Accreditation: North Central Association of Schools and Colleges. www.ncahlc.org

Type of program offered online: Bachelor
Programs accessible to students: Worldwide

Undergraduate tuition per credit hour:
In state – $289.00
Out of state – $289.00

Undergraduate programs offered online:
BS – Agricultural Business
BS – Fire and Emergency Services Administration
BS – Human Development and Family Studies
BA – Liberal Arts

References

Brain Track, An Online College Guide (2010). *Online Education Continues Rapid Growth*. Retrieved 8/28/10 from http://www.braintrack.com/online-colleges/articles/online-education-continues-to-grow

City Town Info Staff (2009). Growth of Online Education Slows, But its Future Remains Rosy. Retrieved 8/29/10 from http://www.citytowninfo.com/career-and-education-news/articles/growth-of-online-education-slows-but-its-future-remains-rosy-09100201

Department of Education (2009). *Evidence-Based Practices in Online Learning: A Meta-Analysis and Review of Online Learning Studies*. Retrieved 8/28/10 from http://www2.ed.gov/about/offices/list/opepd/ppss/reports.html

Eliot, George (Mary Ann Evans 1819-1880). *thinkexist.com*. Retrieved 8/29/10 from http://thinkexist.com/quotes/george_eliot/